ALLYSHIP IN ACTION
WORKBOOK

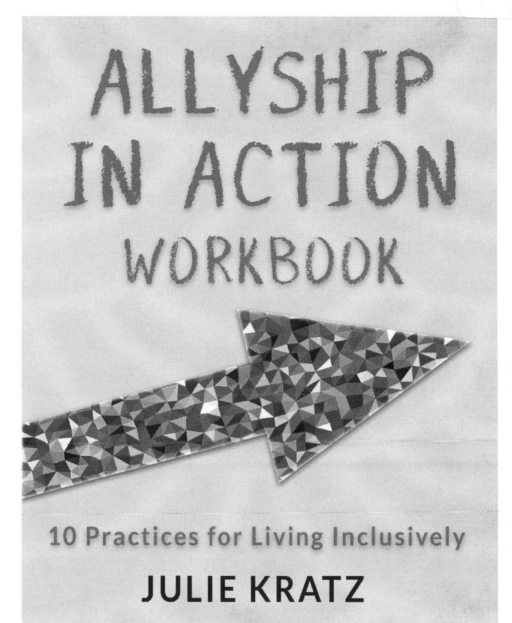

10 Practices for Living Inclusively

JULIE KRATZ

Next Pivot Point
by Julie Kratz

Next Pivot Point Publishing

Books may be ordered through booksellers or by contacting:

Julie Kratz

Next Pivot Point Publishing

julie@nextpivotpoint.com

NextPivotPoint.com

317-525-4310
13470 Shakamac Drive
Carmel, IN 46032

ISBN: 978-1-7365159-6-9 (paperback)
978-1-7365159-7-6 (eBook)

Table of Contents

Other Books by Julie Kratz

Allyship in Action: 10 Practices for Living Inclusively

Pivot Point: How to Build a Winning Career Game Plan

ONE: How Male Allies Support Women for Gender Equality

Lead Like an Ally: A Journey Through Corporate America with Strategies to Facilitate Inclusion

"Little Allies"

"Little Allies Coloring Book"

INTRODUCTION

This activity guide is a companion book to *Allyship in Action: 10 Strategies for Inclusive Living*, designed to lead families, classrooms, and groups to engage in meaningful dialogue about inclusion and allyship.

Use this guide as a tool on your own for development, and then bring your family or group together to help implement inclusive behaviors into your daily lives.

If you're following along with the *Allyship in Action* book, use the chapters as your guide for moving along to the next set of designated chapter activities as you read. Check out the list of additional resources at the conclusion for even more activities, organizations, and ideas.

INTRODUCTION ACTIVITIES

Building Community, Creativity and Critical Thinking with Thoughtful Responses Adult / Instructor Activity

Below is a list of responses that are more beneficial to use in place of "Good job!" or "Great thinking!" As adults/instructors, it can be easy to use the word "good" too often with children. We say things like "Good job!" or "You're being so good," or "That was a great response." While these aren't inherently wrong, they're subjective and conflicting for a child. "Good" and "bad" can mean one thing in one context and something different in another. Children can easily try to learn what your definition of "good" is in order to do exactly what pleases you. When they do this, they are less likely to think outside the box, ask probing questions, disagree, challenge, be creative, or be themselves.

Likewise, when we prescribe thoughts and feelings to a child's behavior that we deem "bad" we don't give them the space to respond with authenticity or autonomy. We say things like, "That wasn't very nice. Apologize!" A child may learn that that specific phrase wasn't "nice" and give a half-hearted apology, but they won't learn what "nice" really sounds like and the apology may not come from a place of understanding and remorse.

Below is a list of responses you can use in place of the more generic ones we tend to use. These responses will hopefully foster an environment where every child is valued, critical thinking is encouraged, and challenge is welcome. These responses will also open the door for the children to be more in charge of the discussion, rather than the children only talking to/responding to you as the instructor. Lastly, these responses will model how to have positive and constructive conversations so that children can continue speaking like this to one another outside of your group time. Children will learn to think critically about the way they treat others, they will be held accountable to that behavior, and they will learn to grow in their communication with others.

When responding positively or fostering deeper discussion:

- "I love how you said . . . because . . ."
- "That is an interesting question. Does anyone have an answer?"
- "What do you think about what _____ just said?"
- "Thanks for offering your opinion. Does anyone agree/disagree? Why?"
- "You explained yourself so clearly. You're helping us understand better."
- "I'm so glad you chimed in with your answer. Without it I don't think we would have thought about it that way."
- "Thanks for saying that in a way that respected what _____ said."
- "Can you explain for us why you said that?"
- "Tell us more about why you think that."
- "I think I understand what you are saying, but can you use an example to explain more so we all understand."
- "I love how _____ shows she is listening by looking at _____ in the eyes when he talks."
- "I love how _____ gently nudged her friend to remind her to listen to her classmate. That was a gentle, yet firm way of holding to our standards as a community."
- "What do you all have to say about what _____ said?"
- "I agree with what you said about _____, but I disagree on _____. I'll explain. . ."
- "I love how you waited to speak until _____ was done speaking. It showed you respected what they had to say and that you don't think you are more important than they are."
- "I like how you said _____ because _____."
- "I never thought about it like that. Thanks for helping me see it in a new way."
- "I appreciate your openness. Now we know how to better care for you."
- "Thanks for being so brave. Your bravery will help us to be more brave."
- "Thanks for being honest. I know it can be really hard to share our honest thoughts, but we are better when we can be honest with one another."
- "What would you like to say to _____ based on what they shared?"

- "Did you all notice how _____ did/said _____? That's an example of (vulnerability/allyship/inclusive language/gratitude/etc.) like we've been talking about."
- "I like how you used the word _____ instead of _____. You're showing us how to be more inclusive."
- "Thanks for showing us how to be understanding of one another. We aren't perfect at all and you showed us how we can be understanding of one another as we stumble and grow together."

When responding to negative situations, here are some ideas:

- "Did you notice how it made _____ feel when you said that?"
- "Why did you choose to say that?"
- "Do you think that what you said helped build _____ up?"
- "Do you think that what you said helped _____ to love themselves?"
- "Do you think that what you said helped _____ to be more courageous?"
- "Do you think that what you said helped all of us to be a better community?"
- "Would an ally say what you just said/do what you did?"
- "When you did that, were you thinking about yourself or thinking about others?"
- "How might you change what you said so that it is more loving?"
- "We know that what you said about _____ isn't true about him/her/them. Tell her what is true so that she can remember that instead."
- "When we hurt others, it's best to apologize so that we can forgive each other. How would you like to apologize to _____?"
- "Hm. You're usually so kind to everyone, but what you said seemed out of character for you. Why is that?"
- "It's not like you to say what you just said. Are you feeling like yourself today?"
- "Usually you're showing others how to listen by looking at me and not being distracted, but today you have been distracted. Can you tell me what's distracting you? Why?"
- "Are you doing/being what you expected from _____? Is it fair to expect something from them that you're not doing yourself?"

- — "How would you like to mend/fix/heal this situation?"
- — "How would you like to make this right?"
- — "What were you feeling when you said/did that? Now that you've had some time/space, would you do it again? Then, how will you make it better for _____?"

Closure Adult / Instructor Activity

Rationale: Have you ever asked a child, "So, what did you learn at school today?" Unless you have a particularly loquacious child, you will usually get something like, "I don't know." Even adults can struggle to recall what they learned after attending a seminar, class or lecture. If we don't implement practices that require us to think about what we have learned, we will easily move on to what becomes more urgent and pressing in our lives. Children are exactly the same way. We have provided these closure activities for kids to take what they have learned with them so that they start to accompany their new knowledge with action. These activities will also help you to gauge where each child is on their ally journey so that you can know how to adapt activities and discussions as you go to meet each child where they are on their journey.

Use the following activities after any/all of the activities in this guide so that your group can process what they learned and take it with them into other contexts within their lives.

Go to https://www.sps186.org/social/?p=125035 or do a Google search for "District 186 Optimistic Closures"

Our Optimistic Closure Activity:

1. Grab a six-sided die.

2. Each number represents an idea of how you will close your activity for the day:

    a. 1: 1 word – have each child write down or say one word they would use to describe what they learned. Allow them to explain or not depending on your preference.

    b. 2: Partners – have children partner up and share how they are feeling after what they learned today. You may use the Emotions Color Wheel to help them name their emotion.

    c. 3: Think, Pair, Share – Have children circle up. Share the phrase, "Now that I know _____, I will _____." And have each of the children fill in the blanks. You may want to provide paper so they can write their thoughts. Give them 30 seconds to a minute to think on their own. Then have them share what they came up with with a person or two next to them. Then have a few (or all) kids share what they said to the group.

    d. 4: Gratitude – Have children circle up. Go around the circle and have each child share something that they are thankful for from the lesson today. Encourage them to thank specific members within the group for something they said or did that helped them learn. You may need to model and then kids will get the hang of the language.

    I.   Ex: "Thank you for being brave and sharing what you did today. It showed me I can be brave too."

    II.   Ex: "Thank you for teaching me about your family. I learned so much about you."

    III.   Ex: "Thank you for listening to me share. I have never shared like that before."

    IV.   Ex: "Thank you for celebrating who I am."

    V.   Ex: "Thank you for teaching me more about the LGBTQ+ community. Now I can learn how to be a better ally."

e.   5: Hands Together – Have children stand in a circle. Focusing on the person to their right (or you can choose left to change it up), they will say one thing they noticed about that person today (encouragement, gratitude, positive affirmation, etc.), grab their hand and squeeze to pass it on. That person will then do the same to the person on their right. It will continue around the circle until every child has said something encouraging about the person to their right and everyone is holding hands. (If you'd rather not have children hold hands, you can have them give a high-five, fist bump, or air-five.)

    i.   If needed, give them these sentence starters to help them say what they're thinking:

        1. "I love how you . . ."

        2. "Thanks for . . ."

        3. "You are so good at . . ."

        4. "I liked when you . . ."

        5. "You taught me . . ."

        6. "You helped me . . ."

f. 6: 60 seconds – Ask children the question, "If you had one minute to share what you learned today with someone who wasn't here, what would you say?" Allow them to prepare their answers. You may need to offer paper for them to write/draw their thoughts. Then, set the timer for 60 seconds and have kids get with a partner and share what they came up with. Make sure you set the timer for 60 seconds again so the second partner can share. Then, say something like: "Remember. Sixty seconds doesn't seem like much, but 60 seconds could change someone's thinking or open the door just enough for big change to happen. Share your 60 seconds with someone today!"

3. As you have time, use one of these closure activities at the end of the day by picking a child to roll the die. Whatever number it lands on will be the closure you do for the day. You typically won't need more than 5 minutes for any of these activities, but make sure you allow all children space to think and time to share.

CHAPTER ONE: WHY

Why Adult / Instructor Activity

Childhood Reflections

Discuss your answers to these questions with a person or two whom you trust:

1. Growing up, what kind of messages did you hear about race/gender/disabilities/LGBTQ+? (colorblindness, boys/ girls do this, etc.)

   a. How did you react to these messages, see others differently, or personally live differently because of them?

2. What problematic statements do you remember yourself or others saying? (retarded, gay as perjorative, etc.)

   a. When did you learn that these statements were harmful? What or who helped you to understand the problems behind these kinds of statements?

3. What exposure did you have to other races, ethnicities, LGBTQ+, people with disabilities, etc.?

   a. What were those exposures like? How did they impact the way you saw those groups of people?

   b. What kind of lived experiences did you not realize or understand until you were an adult? (for example, maybe you didn't realize someone could be gender non-binary until you were an adult because you never got to know someone's experience who was.)

Why Adult / Instructor Activity

Dimensions of Diversity Inventory

What dimensions of diversity do you identify with? Circle or check all that apply to you.

Wealth	Body Size
Rich	Slim
Middle Class	Average
Poor	Large
Language	**Housing**
English-speaking	Owns property
Learned English	Rents property
Non-English/	Homeless
Monolingual	
Mental Health	**Formal Education**
Robust Mental Health	Post-Secondary
Mostly Stable Mental Health	High School
Vulnerable Mental Health	Elementary School
Gender	**Sexuality**
Cisgender Man	Heterosexual
Cisgender Woman	Gay, lesbian, bi, pan, asexual
Trans/intersex/non-binary	
Citizenship	**Neurodiversity**
US Citizen	Neurotypical

Documented US Citizen	Some neuro divergence
Undocumented US Citizen	Significant neurodivergence
Skin Color	**Ability**
White	Non-disabled
Black	Mildly disabled
Brown	Severely disabled

Have a conversation with someone you know personally and with whom you have high trust. Compare dimensions and discuss these questions:

- What identities are most important to you?
- What identities have you felt like you needed to cover or hide?
- What shifted for you when looking at your dimensions?
- What did you learn?

Why Group / Class Activity

Objective: Group members will understand their own dimensions of diversity.

Materials:

— 1-2 pieces of blank white paper per group member.
— Coloring utensils (try to make sure there are different colors for skin color - do a Google search for 'multiracial coloring utensils' and you can purchase online, or look for these in stores.)
— A drawing you (the instructor) created of yourself, with your family, at your home (doesn't need to be anything amazing.)

Directions:

1. Show the group what you drew and explain each part of what you drew so that they can hear your dimensions of diversity clearly. Then, put your drawing away so that group members don't feel like they need to copy off of yours for the activity.

2. Tell the group it's their turn to draw their family the way they want to. Allow them time to draw.

3. Come back together as a group, or have everyone split into partners and discuss these questions:

    a. What do you see that is similar in your drawings?

    b. What do you see that is different in your drawings?

    c. Share your favorite thing about yourself.

    d. Share your favorite thing about your home.

    e. Share something you drew differently than what is true in real life. (refer back to something you may have drawn differently because it's a dimension you've learned to hide or change.)

    f. What did you learn from this activity?

4. Say: "This is just our small group but think about how many other families and people are different than we are. We all have different stories and experiences. Some of us may look similar on the outside, but when we get to know each other, we realize that we all have very different life stories.

Isn't it cool how we are all different? It means that we can learn so much from each other. Imagine how cool it is when we work together, bring our stories, and share our strengths for the common good of others.

But think about how much pain, hurt and brokenness comes when we speak words of hate, when we judge others before getting to know them, when we won't become friends with others, or when we are completely alone. A lot of the world is experiencing those things. How does that make you feel to know that? (Have a few students share their answers). That's why I'm so glad we are learning together.

We want to become allies. An ally is someone who stands up for others and is a friend to others–even if no one else around them is. It's hard work to become an ally because the rest of the world is often doing the opposite. We want to become allies to the people who are often pushed to the side, forgotten, lonely, hurt, judged, and mistreated. We'll spend the next few weeks learning how to do that, but honestly, it's a life-long process to learn how to show up for others."

CHAPTER TWO: EMPATHY

Empathy Adult / Instructor Activity

Self-Reflection & Practice with Empathy

1. Watch the Brene Brown on Sympathy vs. Empathy video (To find this video, do a search on YouTube for '*Brene Brown sympathy empathy*')

2. Reflect on these questions through journaling or discussing with a trusted person in your life:

   a. What situations/circumstances/people groups are easier for you to empathize with? (For example, you may be able to empathize with someone who battles chronic illness because you do as well.)

   b. What situations/circumstances/people groups often elicit a sympathetic response from you rather than an empathetic response? Why do you think that is?

   c. What is difficult about practicing empathy in your relationships? What about with strangers?

3. Practice. Keep these simple questions "in your back pocket" to help you empathize with others or start conversations that will elicit an empathetic connection.

   a. "How are you *really* doing with _____" (situation/circumstance/relationship/ event/etc.)

   b. "What has been on your mind lately?" Another way to word it may be, "what has been causing you the most stress lately?"

   c. "What do you wish people understood about you/your situation/your life/etc."

Empathy Group / Class Activity

Objective: Group members will understand that everyone has a different perspective and that our experiences and beliefs shape our perspectives of others.

Materials:

The following images (printed or on given slideshow)

— Perspective (To find images, do a Google search for 'duck or rabbit image' or 'inkblot images.')

Directions:

1. Show each of the images to the group and give the directions: "Look at this image and don't tell me what you see just yet. Just look at it and we will share what we see."

2. Show each image for about 30 seconds.

3. Ask: "What do you see?"

4. Make sure each person gets a chance to answer. Point out similarities and differences between what each child sees. Let them openly react to the differences between what they see.

5. **Discuss:** (Make sure to pause after each question to allow the students to discuss their thoughts.)

    a. "Isn't it interesting how we can all look at the same picture, but see completely different things? Why do you think it is that we see different things? Is it a bad thing that we see different things? Is there one right way to see things? Explain."

    b. "How does this apply to looking at people around us? What makes us see people differently?"

    c. "What happens when we see people differently? How are you seeing this play out in the world today?"

Empathy Group / Class Activity

Objective: Group members will discuss their similarities and differences with another person in the group so that they can relate to their similarities and appreciate their differences.

Materials:

- Big piece of paper/posterboard (if unavailable, use 3+ pieces of regular paper.)
- Coloring utensils (make sure there are different options for different skin colors.)

Directions:

1. Split the group into groups of 2,

2. Pass out one big piece of paper for each group.

3. Have them draw a Venn Diagram or T chart with 3 columns.

4. Say: "On one side write the name of one of your group members. In the middle, write the word 'same,' and on the other side write the name of your other group member. Now, I am going to ask you some questions and you are going to talk about your answers and then draw them where they need to go on your chart. For example, I might say, 'What color are your eyes?' and if you have the same eye color, you can draw eyes with your eye color in the 'Same' category. If you have different eye colors, you can each draw your eyes in the category that has your name in it."

5. Work through these questions slowly enough for students to draw their answers. You may want to have a way to display 2-3 questions at a time so people can eventually work at their own pace.

   a. What color are my eyes?

   b. What color is my hair?

   c. What color is my skin?

   d. Where do I live? (house, apartment, etc.)

   e. Where was I born?

   f. What language(s) do I speak?

   g. What is my gender?

   h. What is my ethnicity?

   i. How tall am I?

      j.   Who lives in my house?

      k. What do my parents look like?

      l.   What do I like to do for fun?

      m. Feel free to add any questions you think would be fitting.

6. Walk around the room and engage in conversation about what everyone is drawing and what they are learning.

7. Once everyone finishes drawing their answers, discuss as a group: "What was surprising about this activity? What did you learn?"

8. Say: "We have a lot more in common than we may have realized. But we also learned that it isn't wrong to talk about our differences with each other. When we acknowledge differences, we can do so in a respectful way that admires differences rather than points to them as something that is bad or makes someone less than."

Empathy Group / Class Activity

Objective: Group members will learn the power of taking a different perspective.

Materials:

— <u>Blue Eyes vs. Brown Eyes video</u> (go to YouTube and search "Jane Elliott 'Blue Eyes - Brown Eyes' Experiment Anti-Racism.")

Directions:

Show this video to your group.

1. Once the video is finished, discuss with your group:

2. How do you think you would have reacted if you were in this classroom?

    a. Why do you think there were a lot of people who said this experiment was bad?

    b. How do you think kids would react if we did a similar experiment today?

    c. Can you think of another way we could teach kids the same ideas?

CHAPTER THREE: VULNERABILITY

Vulnerability Adult / Instructor Activity

Shame Triggers Exercise

1. In order for us to show up vulnerably, we need to recognize where shame can keep us hiding from vulnerable moments. Take a look at the list below. Circle the ones that can or have been a shame trigger for you:

   a. Irrelevance

   b. being called a racist/sexist/bad person

   c. making mistakes

   d. not having the answers

   e. being wrong

   f. have to unlearn or relearn something

   g. reckoning with discomfort

   h. rumbling in uncertainty

   i. lack of clear path forward

   j. ticking someone off

2. Reflect on where these triggers show up for you (conversations, situations, relationships, etc.)

3. Grab a journal or piece of paper. Write down your top three shame triggers on the left side of the paper. On the right side, write down the truth and/or an action that will help you to manage that shame trigger so that you can show up vulnerably for yourself and other people.

a. Example:

Making mistakes causes me to feel shame	No one is perfect and everyone is learning. I am allowed to make mistakes and learn from them so that I can move forward. When I make a mistake, I am willingly showing others that I am not perfect and that I am learning too. That gives people the space to make mistakes around me. This creates a space for vulnerability and authenticity, which creates connection.

Vulnerability Group / Class Activity

Objective: Group members will uncover biases they have and learn that anyone can be a leader.

Materials:

— Blank paper
— Coloring utensils

Directions:

1. Hand each group member a piece of paper and coloring utensils.

2. Say: "Draw a picture of a leader." Do not give extra directions or context. Let them go with the prompt based on their own thoughts.

3. Say: "Everyone hold up your picture of your leader. What similarities do you notice? What differences do you notice?"

4. Use some of the similarities and differences you saw to ask the following questions. For example, if majority of the group drew males, ask them why they all chose to draw a male. If one person drew a person of color, ask that student why they drew a person of color.

   a. "Why did you draw what you did?"
   b. "Why did you choose that race/skin color for a leader?"
   c. "Why did you choose that gender for a leader?"
   d. "Why is your leader wearing that?"

5. As you discuss the answers to these questions, you may begin uncovering biases or prejudices that people have against certain genders/races/socio-economic backgrounds/etc. Allow them to have a safe space to talk about their biases and start to discuss how those biases can change. If you don't know what to say, continue to ask "why" questions to get them to explain their thinking.

6. Say: "I'm glad we got to do this together. Even though we realized that we have some negative views of certain kinds of people, we were able to be honest and open and share without the fear of judgment. Now that it's in the open, we can learn to think differently. Anyone can be a leader. We might not have come to that conclusion if we hadn't had this open conversation together."

Vulnerability Group/Class Activity

Objective: Group members will learn about how we all make assumptions about other people based on our biases, lived experiences, and background knowledge.

Materials:

— This video on assumptions kids make about each other (Search on YouTube for "What Assumptions Do Kids Make About Each other? | Reverse Assumptions" There are a few videos that are the same style just with different kids, so feel free to choose any of them.)
— 3 pieces of paper per kid
— Coloring utensils with a wide range of color options
— 3 pictures of different kids (try to find a black girl, a LGBTQ+ of a different race than white, and a white boy.)

Directions:

1. Say: "Today we are going to talk about 'assumptions.' Assumptions are ideas we guess about people based on what we know or see, but not usually based on any kind of truth. For example, you may believe that people in California are all rich because you've only met one person from California and they lived in a big, nice house. So if a new kid walked into your class and said they were from California, you may *assume* that they are rich–even though you don't know anything about the new kid. We actually do this all of the time without realizing it.
We assume things about people without getting to know them. Sometimes we assume things based on our limited experiences. Sometimes we assume based on a little bit of information we have. And other times we assume based on negative opinions we have about certain people. We are going to watch a video that shows how kids just like you can assume things about other kids based on what they hear."

2. Show the video to your group.

3. Discuss the following questions:

    a. What did you think about the video?
    b. What was surprising to you about their assumptions?
    c. Why do you think they assumed some of the things they did?

4. Say: "Now we are going to try something similar to the video we just watched. I am going to read a few sentences that describe a kid and as I read, you will draw what you think this

kid looks like. Then, I will show you what the kid looks like and we will talk about the differences between what you drew and what is true."

    a. I'm 8 years old and I love to skateboard. I've been skateboarding ever since I was only 5 years old. My dad taught me how because he's a professional skateboarder. I want to be professional when I get older too. I love the weekends because I get to go to the skatepark with him and learn new tricks.

        i. Show them the picture of the black girl.
       ii. Discuss: "How is your drawing similar to the real picture of this girl? How is it different? Why did you draw what you did? What did she say in her description that made you draw what you did?" (Allow kids to openly discuss their assumptions and biases.)

    b. I'm 10 years old and my favorite thing to do is read. I would read all day if my teachers would let me. Usually my math teacher has to take my book away because I'll just read instead of focus on my math work. When I grow up I want to be a writer so that I can write books that kids like me want to read.

        i. Show them the picture of the LGBTQ kid
       ii. Discuss: "How is your drawing similar to the real picture of this child? How is it different? Why did you draw what you did? What did they say in their description that made you draw what you did?" (Allow kids to openly discuss their assumptions and biases.)

    c. I'm 12 years old and I love to sing and dance. I act in a lot of plays too. I hope that I can be the lead role in a broadway musical one day. I get to go to New York this summer to see Hairspray, which is my favorite musical ever. If I can't be on Broadway, I'd love to be in the New York City Ballet when I get older.

        i. Show them the picture of the white boy
       ii. Discuss: "How is your drawing similar to the real picture of this child? How is it different? Why did you draw what you did? What did he say in his description that made you draw what you did?" (Allow kids to openly discuss their assumptions and biases.)

5. Discuss: "What did you learn from today's activities? What are some negative thoughts or opinions you realized you had about certain people/certain interests? What do you want to start to do differently after this lesson today?"

CHAPTER FOUR: CURIOSITY

Curiosity Adult / Instructor Activity

Bias Inventory

1. Take at least two assessments from the Harvard Implicit Association Test (To find this test, do a Google search for *'harvard implicit bias test.'*)

2. What did you learn about your own biases?

3. What biases did you have that you didn't realize you had?

4. Where/how do you think these biases have formed in your life?

5. Compare notes with someone else. What shifted for both of you?

Curiosity Group / Class Activity

Objective: Group members will become more observant of their books and toys and start to learn how to have conversations about how to welcome diversity.

Materials:

— All the toys and childrens' books in your group's area or in your household
— Piece of paper per group (if splitting into groups)
— Writing utensils
— Big blank piece of paper/whiteboard
— Two different color writing utensils for whiteboard/big piece of paper

Directions:

1. On the whiteboard or big blank piece of paper, write down the following categories with room for tally marks: boy, girl, white, BIPOC, American, ethnic, non-disabled, disabled.

2. Pass out a piece of paper and a writing utensil for each group (or give one to each person if you aren't splitting into groups.)

3. Say: "Write down exactly what I wrote down on your piece of paper. We're going to work together to try to find what different people groups are represented in our books. We have categories that we wrote on this paper. BIPOC means 'Black, Indigenious, and People of Color' and ethnic means someone that would be from a different country. We're going to flip through our books and put a tally for each category we see. Most of the time a character will get more than one tally. Like we might find a boy that is BIPOC and non-disabled, so we will give a tally for each category. Even though a character will appear in more than one page, just do the tally marks for that character once."

4. Have group members gather all of the books or hand out a few books to each individual/group.

5. If group members are doing this independently, say: "You will flip through your books and write a tally mark for each category that you find. Then we will come together and write all of our tallies on a scoresheet or the whiteboard together."

6. If your group members are working on teams, say: "You will write down your tallies on your group's piece of paper. Assign one person to write the tallies. They will be the Tally Marker while the others are looking in the books and telling the Tally Marker where to put their tallies."

7. Once students are finished, come back together to collect each individual's/group's tallies.

8. Now, do the same thing with toys if your classroom or household has toys.

9. Choose a different color writing utensil and add the tallies to our totals.

10. **Discuss:**

    a. "What are you noticing when you look at these tallies?"
    b. "Why do you think that is?"
    c. "Who seems to be missing from our toys and books?"
    d. "Why do you think that is?"
    e. "How can we change that?"

Curiosity Adult / Instructor Activity

What We Don't Know Exercise

1. On a scale of 1-10, 1 being you don't know anything and 10 being you feel very knowledgeable, rate your level of understanding of the following dimensions of diversity:

   a. Race

   b. Gender

   c. LGBTQ+

   d. Ethnicity

   e. Disability

   f. Poverty

   g. Multiculturalism

   h. Gender Non-binary

   i. Religion

   j. Systemic Racism

2. Process these questions and discuss with a trusted friend:

   a. In the past, what has held you back from learning about these different dimensions?

   b. How might you improve your understanding of other dimensions of diversity?

   c. What are some actions you can take to learn more? (Listen to podcasts, join a club, read a book, etc.)

Curiosity Adult / Instructor Activity

Curious Questions Brainstorming

1. Reflect on some of the following questions designed to help you stay curious. Then, answer the following questions through journaling, talking with a trusted friend, or some other form of reflection you find to be useful and productive.

   Questions Help Us Stay Curious

   a. What is possible?
   b. What is the wildest idea we could come up with?
   c. What perspective are we missing?
   d. Who haven't we heard from?
   e. What skills do we want to learn?

2. What questions do you like the most?

3. How could you ask these questions more often?

4. What holds you back from asking curious questions?

5. Compare notes with a friend and take turns asking curious questions in an actual conversation.

Curiosity Class / Group Activity

Objective: Kids will grow their curiosity in regards to different dimensions of diversity.

Materials:

- 10 large pieces of paper
  - Write one of the following on its own page:
    - Race, gender, LGBTQ+, ethnicity, disability, poverty, multiculturalism, gender-neutral, religion, systemic racism
  - Write "Think | Wonder" in a T-chart
- Writing utensils

Directions:

1. Place the 10 pieces of paper spread out across the room.

2. Say: "Today we are going to explore what makes us all unique and different. There is probably a lot we don't understand about what makes people different. So, today we are going to explore what we know and talk about what we would like to understand better. It's ok to ask questions to seek understanding, but it's never ok to ask questions with the intentions of hurting or making fun of another person or group of people."

3. Say: "Look around the room. There are 10 pieces of paper that have different words on them that may describe what makes people unique on the outside, on the inside, or have different experiences than you have. At our own pace, we are going to walk around the room and visit each piece of paper. On the "Think" side, you will write anything you think you know about that word. You can add what you think or experiences you've had. On the "Wonder" side. You'll write anything you're wondering or curious about. You can ask questions that you would like to know. We will have plenty of time to talk about this after we are done, so as you walk around be silent so that we can all work independently until we are ready to come together."

4. It may be best to model what it looks like to add your thoughts and questions. Here is an idea you can use to model. Grab the paper with "Multiculturalism" and say: "So, I know that 'multi' means 'many' because there are words like 'multicolored' which means many colors. So I'm going to write 'multi means many' on the 'Think' side." Then, grab the 'Systemic Racism' paper and say: "I know that 'racism' means intentionally thinking or doing hurtful things to someone because of their race. So I'll write that under the 'Think' side. I'm not

sure what systemic means though, so I'll write 'what is systemic? It looks like the word "system" so maybe it has to do with systems?'"

5. Depending on the group, you may want to do a few together as a class before sending the kids to write their own. It can be helpful to draw branches off of kids' answers to show how their thinking or questions branches off of what is already written. For example, one kid may say 'boy and girl' for 'Gender' and another child may say 'some people don't identify as either boy or girl' so you can draw a branch off of 'boy and girl' and write that. This can create a visual web for the group to see.

6. Give each group member a writing utensil and have them walk around the room at their own pace.

7. When they are done, bring the group back together and discuss these questions:

    a. What was difficult about this activity?

    b. What was helpful about this activity?

    c. What did you learn?

    d. What are you still wondering?

8. Say: "Obviously, there is still a lot to learn. What we did today was supposed to spark curiosity and help us ask questions, but we won't get all of the answers right away. In fact, we will be continually learning about these terms and expanding our knowledge. In fact, a lot of adults like me are still learning and growing in this area. Thanks for being vulnerable with your questions and giving each other space to be open and honest about what we think we know and what we really don't know. I can't wait to learn more together."

Curiosity Group/Class Activity

Objective: The group will use their curiosity to learn more about different dimensions of diversity.

Materials:

— The 10 pieces of paper from the previous activity
— Dimensions of Diversity terms list (below)
— This is to help you define the terms as you and the group discuss

Dimensions of Diversity Terms List

- *Diversity*: Different groups of people (i.e. gender, race, ethnicity, sexual orientation, abilities.)
- *Inclusion*: A sense of belonging for diverse groups of people.
- *Majority group*: The group that generally holds the largest amount of power in society and in workplaces (i.e. white, straight, male, cisgender, non-disabled.)
- *Underrepresented groups*: The groups that fall outside of the majority group by one or more factors (non-white, LGBTQ+, female, gender non-binary, disabled.)
- *Intersectionality*: The intersection of more than one marker of diversity (i.e. race + gender, disabled + gay.)
- *Gender non-binary*: A category for those that identify outside of the masculine or feminine gender boxes (synonym: gender-neutral.)
- *Cisgender*: A category for those that identify their gender with the gender or sex they were assigned at birth.
- *LGBTQ+*: An acronym that represents lesbian, gay, bisexual, transgender, queer and those that identify with other markers of difference in sexual orientation and/or gender.
- *People of color*: People that identify as non-white.
- *White fragility*: White people's aversion to talking about race or apathy towards racism's existence.
- *White supremacy*: The belief that the white race is superior to other races.
- *Disabilities*: Physical or non-physical differences from the majority group (i.e. mental health, limited mobility, visually impaired.)
- *Privilege*: The advantages one has over others based on their associations with the majority group (i.e. white, straight, male, cisgender, non-disabled.)
- *Ally*: One that leverages their privilege to help others that are underrepresented (i.e. mentor, sponsor, advocate, coach, challenger.)
- *Unconscious bias*: The beliefs that one holds that they are often unaware about those that are underrepresented.

- *Mansplaining*: Traditional male behavior that minimizes women by over or underexplaining something based on assumptions about gender.
- *Whitesplaining*: Traditional white behavior that minimizes people of color by assuming they know what it means to be a person of color.
- *Gender equality*: The belief that all genders of humans are equal and should be treated equally.

Directions:

1. This activity may need to take more than one day depending on how conversations go. The goal is to take the 10 pieces of paper from the last activity and talk about what the kids thought they knew about each one and what they are curious about.

2. One at a time, pull a piece of paper out and do the following with each one:

   a. Read what everyone wrote.

   b. Ask: "What do you think of what was written?"

   c. Read the questions the kids wrote.

   d. Ask: "Can anyone answer these questions?"

   e. Ask: "What are some ways we can get answers to these questions or learn more?"

   f. Give answers to any of their questions that the group cannot answer. Take time to help them define the terms they did not know.

CHAPTER FIVE: EMOTIONS

Emotions Adult / Instructor Activity

Visualization Exercise

One of the ways you can show up as an ally in all aspects of your life is to start to visualize yourself doing just that. The more we visualize ourselves doing something, the more we can start to implement the small habits that turn into a lifestyle.

1. Grab a journal or device for you to write down your thoughts.

2. Visualize yourself leading like an ally in all aspects of your life. It might help to write down the major areas of your life such as work, home, friendships, etc.

3. Write down everything that comes to mind without worrying about what you are saying or how you are saying it. Keep it your most honest thoughts.

4. How could you start implementing small actions or habits to make your vision a reality? Write down some thoughts for each area of your life.

Emotions Adult / Instructor Activity

Personal Value Proposition Exercise

Being an ally can be draining because it is often work that can only be done when you are swimming up stream. When you are emotionally spent and wanting to give up, it's important to have an anchor of truth that brings you back to the mission. For this exercise you will create a personal value proposition. This can be used every day, but especially in the times when being an ally brings tough emotions. Furthermore, a personal value proposition is tied to your own purpose and identity so that you can more clearly hold to your personal ally vision.

1. Set a clear goal for yourself as an ally.

2. Make a list of strengths you have – no matter if you think they relate specifically to DEI work or not.

3. Make a list of your passions. What gets you engaged or "fired up"?

4. Make a list of what is unique about you.

5. Brainstorm ways your strengths, passions and uniqueness can intersect with your goal. This is your personal value proposition (PVP).

6. Take what you've brainstormed and make it more clear and concise to reflect your PVP.

7. Then, do this exercise with a friend and talk about your unique PVPs.

Emotions Group / Class Activity

Objective: Group members will learn how to identify, talk about, and work through their emotions.

Materials:

— Emotions color wheel (To find this, do a Google search for 'emotions color wheel' - there will be a lot of options so just select the one that works best for your group!)
— You may want to make a copy for each group member so you can reference it later or even have them take it home.
— Whiteboard or big piece of paper.
— A children's book of your choice that features characters that experience different emotions throughout the story.

Directions:

1. Say: "We are going to be talking about emotions today. Let's name some emotions together. As you name them, I'll write them down."

2. Point to one of the emotions and ask: "What are some other words you can think of for this emotion? For example, another way to say 'happy' is 'joyful' so I'll add that as a branch off of 'happy.' What else can you think of for these emotions?"

3. Write down the words they come up with as branches off of the first emotions they came up with.

4. Pull out the Emotions Color Wheel.

5. Say: "This wheel names even more emotions that we might not have even thought of. Point to an emotion and tell me about a time you felt that." (Try to get an answer from each member of the group.)

6. Point to an emotion and discuss: "What does this emotion feel like? What does it look like? Have you experienced this? When? What do you do when you feel that way? What can you do more or less of in those situations?"

7. Pull out the children's book you chose.

8. Say: "We're going to read this book together as a group. As we read, I'm going to stop and we will discuss what kind of emotions the characters seem to be feeling. We'll also talk about how they seem to be handling their emotions."

- As you read, stop and ask these questions when you see that they can fit and allow the group to discuss:
  - What emotion do you think they are feeling? How can you tell?
  - What do you think caused them to feel that emotion?
  - What should they do to handle their emotions?
  - Do you think they should have done something differently? Why?
  - What would you do if you were in this character's situation? How would you feel?

Bonus: Now that you have talked about emotions and the Emotions Wheel, use it in real time with your group when they're experiencing big emotions. Try this conversation:

- Reassure and validate. It might sound something like, "Everyone experiences all kinds of emotions. Kids and adults. Emotions aren't a bad thing. Sometimes our emotions can make us act in a way that we didn't intend, but that's why it's important to talk about them in a safe space. We always want to learn from our emotions."
- "Can you point [on the color wheel] to which emotion you were feeling when it happened?"
- "What were you thinking when it happened?"
- "What did you do? Is that what you meant to do?"
- "How would you handle it differently next time?"
- You may want to model processing emotions by telling your group about an event that happened to you that day and how you were feeling based on the Emotions Wheel.

CHAPTER SIX: COURAGE

Courage Adult / Instructor Activity

Your Implicit Biases

When we come into contact with confusing, unclear or unfamiliar information, we try to make sense of it based on what we already know. This is how implicit bias happens. When we come into contact with something new, different, or confusing, we quickly make unconscious associations in our minds, even when we don't mean to.

For this exercise, see how your brain makes sense of the given confusing information. Try to read the sentences below:

If you can raed tihs it is bceuase our mndis hvae laenred how to put tgoehter new or ucnlaer ifnmoramtoin in a way taht is esay to mkae snsee of bsaed on the cnotxet gvien. Our mndis are albe to do tihs wtihuot our concsuios cnrotol.

Now read this version:

If you can read this it is because our minds have learned how to put together new or unclear information in a way that is easy to make sense of based on the context given. Our minds are able to do this without our conscious control.

This exercise was adapted from: <u>The Kirwan Institute for the Study of Race and Ethnicity, The Ohio State University</u>

Reflect:

When you come into contact with something or someone new or different, what are you thinking? What unconscious associations are your mind making? Pay attention to your thoughts this week that may reveal implicit bias.

Courage Group / Class Activity

Objective: Group members will learn how to identify microaggressions and respond as an ally.

Materials:

The Scenarios 1-5 from the directions below written on pieces of paper to hand out to groups.

Directions:

1. In this activity you will teach your group about microaggressions. Then, group members will act out scenarios where a microaggression happens and they will show what you can do in the situation when you witness a microaggression taking place.

2. Say: "We're going to learn a new word today. Microaggressions (write it on a whiteboard or piece of paper). Let's break it down. (Underline 'micro') Can anyone guess what 'micro' means? 'Micro' means small. (Underline 'aggressions') Can anyone guess what 'aggressions' means? What about the word 'aggressive'? A microaggression is a small comment, joke, or phrase that is hurtful or harmful to someone based on their race, ethnicity, gender, religion, ability, etc. Usually the person saying it thinks it is normal to say it or that it isn't a big deal to say it. But it is hurtful to the other person. I'm going to present some scenarios to you so that we can all understand what a microaggression may sound like."

3. Present the following scenarios to the group and talk about what they would do if they were in this situation. Here are some questions to ask:
    a. What do you think about this situation?
    b. Is it wrong to do/say what they did? Why or why not?
    c. What would you do if you saw this happen?

4. Scenario 1: A white student in a classroom says to a black student: "You're smarter than the other black kids in this class."

5. Scenario 2: A boy says to a girl: "You can't play with that toy. It's for boys."

6. Scenario 3: Your friend says to a stranger in a wheelchair: "What happened to your leg?"

7. Scenario 4: A group of white kids says to a new kid who is mexican: "You can't sit with us. You don't belong."

8. Scenario 5: A white girl says to a black girl: "Can I touch your hair?"

9. Say: "Now that we've discussed a few examples of microaggressions, we are going to practice being an ally if we were in these situations. You're going to get into groups of 3 and each of you will get one of the scenarios we just discussed. One person will be the person saying the microaggression, one of you will be the victim of the microaggression, and one of you will play the ally. You are going to act out the microaggression, and then act out what it would look like to be an ally in that situation. Remember, we never want to say these things in real life to other people. This activity is just to practice how to be an ally and stand up for others when you hear microaggressions happening around you."

10. Allow the groups time to practice their scenarios. Walk around to each group and ask to see what they've come up with so that you can field their act before allowing them to perform in front of the group.

11. Have each group perform their act.

12. **Discuss:** "What did you learn from today's activity? What are some things you can do to be an ally to people around you who are experiencing microaggressions?"

CHAPTER SEVEN: COACHING

Coaching Group / Class Activity

Objective: Group members will learn how to speak positive affirmations to themselves.

Materials:

- A list of positive words you would use to describe yourself and an affirmation or mantra using some or all of those words (you will use this as an example for the group members.)
- Paper
- Writing utensils
  - You may want to get "fancier" paper/writing utensils if you want group members to hang this up in their homes, or if you will hang it in a classroom or shared space.

Directions:

1. The goal of this activity is to help your group members learn how to speak positive affirmations or repeat a positive mantra to themselves consistently. You will help individuals come up with one together and talk about ways they can implement it into their daily routine.

2. Pass out a blank piece of paper to each group member (not the fancy paper yet, this is just for brainstorming!).

3. Say: "We want to help each other come up with what we call 'positive affirmations' or a 'mantra'. A mantra is kind of like a statement that you repeat frequently because you want to live by it. Positive affirmations are positive, encouraging and true things we say to ourselves to remind us of who we are. Why do you think it's important to create mantras or positive affirmations?"

4. Say: "On your piece of paper, write down words you would use to describe yourself. If you're having a hard time thinking, ask people around you what they would say. Remember to keep it positive because we want this to be an environment where people are welcome, encouraged, built up, and safe."

5. If any people respond with a negative word, here are some ideas for how to respond:

    a. If the person said something negative about themselves: "It can be hard sometimes to believe good things about ourselves. I sometimes think negative things about myself too. But they aren't true. And what you said isn't true either. That's why we want to talk about what is true so we can speak it over ourselves every day and live more like who we really are."

    b. If a person said something negative about another group member: "We would never want our place to be an unsafe or hurtful place, but when you said that you made it unsafe and hurtful. What you said isn't true, because _____. We only want to speak what is true and encouraging to each other. Even if you were joking, it can be harmful. So try again. What is something positive you can say to describe that person?"

6. Walk around the room and make sure everyone has positive descriptors written.

7. Say: "Now that we have ideas of what to write, we're going to turn this into a sentence or phrase. (Show and explain your example). You can keep using your piece of paper and the help of friends around you to come up with yours."

8. Say: "Now we are going to make these more fun and permanent so that you can take yours home and display it somewhere where you can read it every day."

9. Pass out the fun paper, writing utensils, etc.

10. As group members are working, discuss ways they can implement this into their daily routine. Here are a few ideas:

    a. Post it on a mirror.
    b. Hang it on the fridge.
    c. Create a chant or "call back" with a friend or someone in their family. One person says, "You are–" and the other says, "smart!" And you work through the list of words that way.
    d. For older children, you can encourage them to journal before bed. Have them write down when they felt bad and then cross it off or throw it away and write what is true.

Coaching Group / Class Activity

Materials:

— A printed or drawn dice template (to find a template, do a Google search for 'blank dice template')
— Coloring utensils
— Scissors
— Tape or glue

Directions:

1. In this activity group members will be creating a 6-sided die for each member that represents what each child loves to do. You will use this die to create fun experiences for each other and to teach group members to listen to each other and care for each other.

2. Say: "Have you ever made someone's day before? Have you ever gotten to plan a gift, surprise or activity for someone? What was that like?

   a. "Well, today, we are going to create a fun way to make someone's day. We are going to create dice. Each of you will have a die that has six different things on it that would make your day. The trick is, you will be creating one for your partner–not your own. This will be just like the dice you would roll when you play a game, except our dice will have pictures of things that we love or things that would make our day. We'll use these dice to roll when we want to pick something kind to do for someone else that you know they would love.

   b. "I'm going to split you into groups of 2 and you are going to ask each other questions, but make sure you listen really well. Their answers are going to help you draw on the die. We have to listen to each other to find out what would make their day a great day."

3. Start with the first person and give the other people the list of questions:

   a. Think about the best day in your life. What was it like?
   b. What would make your day the best?
   c. What have your best days been like?
   d. What were you doing?
   e. Who were you with?
   f. How did you feel?
   g. Since some of what the kids talk about may not be doable in your context, feel free to add other questions that would work with your context.

        i. Ex: What is your favorite toy to play with here? What is your favorite game to play here? What is your favorite snack to eat here?

4. Say: "Ok, I hope you listened well because you are going to make your partner's die. Write their name on one side, and then you need to think of 5 things that they said would make their day. Then you will draw them on the die. So, what kinds of things would make their day the best?"
5. Allow them time to make the dies. You will probably also need to show them how to cut them out and put them together.

6. Ask: "What was difficult about this? Was it hard to really listen to the other person?"

7. Say: "It can be really difficult to listen to someone else. A lot of times we just want to make the conversation all about us. But today we had to focus on the other person. But wasn't it fun? It will be fun when we get to roll the dice to pick something to do to make their day, too. If we do stuff like this in our group, we can learn to do it everywhere we go in all of our relationships."

8. Periodically, have a child grab a die and roll it so that the class can do something for that child, or that single child can do something for another. You could have each child grab a die to roll so they're all doing something at once, or focus on one kid at a time.

CHAPTER EIGHT: ACCOUNTABILITY

Accountability Adult / Instructor Activity

Network Diversity Dimensions Inventory

1. Write down the names of the top 10 people you spend the most time with. Look through your phone, emails, calendar, wherever you communicate with people.

2. Categorize your top 10 by the following categories: gender, ethnicity, age, socioeconomic status, part of the country, profession, physical ability, and any other category that comes to mind.

3. Process these questions on your own and with a trusted friend:

    a. What are you noticing about the people you spend time with?
    b. How has your network ended up looking like it does?
    c. What/who is missing from a representation perspective?
    d. Who could you spend more time with?
    e. How could you diversify your network?

Accountability Group / Class Activity

Objective: Group members will create materials that help them continue the work of allyship in their lives.

Materials:

- Be creative with how you do this so that it fits your group's routine. Here are some ideas:
  - Corkboard
  - Jar(s)
  - Blackboard/whiteboard
  - Fun paper
  - String
  - Hole puncher(s)
  - Frames

Directions:

1. Explain to the group that we want to connect everything they've been learning about allyship and inclusive behaviors with the rest of their lives. Explain that they will be creating a personal journal that they will use, as well as an interactive board that you all will use to plan and create vision and purpose with bringing allyship into all aspects of their lives–including the lives of the people around them. You want to be a facilitator as much as possible and let the rest of the group take the lead on this.

2. Start with the journal: you can choose how these will be designed, but an easy way to do this is to grab a few pieces of paper, fold them in half, hole punch the edges, and use string to hold it together. Pass out the materials for the journals.

3. Explain how to put the journals together.

4. Page 1: Invitation

   a. Discuss: "Let's think of someone in our lives who you want to know about what you've been learning. How can you share with them?"
   b. "Once you've chosen your person, draw their picture, write their name, and write a sentence or two about why you want to share with them. Leave the right hand page blank so that you can write down your progress with that person. You can write down any conversations you've had or experiences you've had together."

5. As group members are working on this page, talk about the following questions they can use to talk to this person about what they're learning.
    a. What do you want to know more about?
    b. What is holding you back from knowing more or doing more?
    c. Talk about how to share the activities you've been doing in your group.

6. Page 2: Organizations
    a. Brainstorm or talk about organizations that support diversity, equity and inclusion. Have the group pick the organization that they're most passionate about.
    b. Discuss: "Which organization sounds like one you'd like to support or donate to this month? What are other ways we could support organizations besides giving money?"
    c. Write the name of the organization on the left side of the page and then write a goal for how you will personally support them. Whether that's a goal for how much money you want to raise or a goal to do something else for the organization. Leave the right hand page blank so you can write down your progress from your goal."

7. Page 3: School
    a. Discuss: "What are some ways you can bring what you've learned into your school?"
    b. "Draw a picture of what it would look like if everyone in your group was an ally to everyone else. Write down your goal for yourself for how you will bring what you've learned into your group. Just like we've been doing, leave the right side page blank so you can journal about your progress."

8. Pages 4+

    a. Leave these blank to be used later on. Encourage the group members to journal about their ongoing experience with learning to be an ally.

9. Bring everyone back to together to begin the full group activity.

10. Say: "Now we want to talk about how we can hold our group accountable to staying active in our work as an ally. One of the ways we will do that is to raise money together to go to an organization of our choice. You each picked an organization that you want to personally support, and that is awesome. It will be great to take that home and get your family and friends on board with supporting that organization. But we will pick one as a class and work on raising money together. This jar is where we can keep our group donations so we can keep track of how much we have."

    a. Keep the jar in a place where everyone can see, and keep the total written and updated often.

    b.   Another idea is to have group members write letters to workers in that organization so that you can give the letters and the money when you donate.

11. If an election is coming up, pick a place to write down the name of one candidate that is running. Talk about ways you can learn about this candidate together. Change the name of the candidate every week so your group is learning about someone new together.

    a.   If the election is coming up and there are candidates that would be important to have on the school board in order to support diversity, equity and inclusion, then you could have everyone create posters encouraging others to vote for that person.

    b.   Discuss as a group how they can support these candidates–even as children.

12. Pick a time of day to consistently talk about their journals, the donation jar, and the candidate of the day/week. Take time to refer back to these on a regular basis (even if it is brief) to keep the work of allyship ongoing.

CHAPTER NINE: PRIVILEGE

Privilege Adult / Instructor Activity

Privilege Exercise

1. Complete the following Privilege exercise. The purpose of this activity is getting a better understanding of your sources of privilege and those that you know. Privilege is not a bad thing; it is a chance to be an ally for someone different than you. Many items on this list are excerpted and adapted with permission from *Better Allies: Everyday Actions to Create Inclusive, Engaging Workplaces* by Karen Catlin

   For each statement, put a + sign if you agree, or a – sign if you disagree. Tally your total + signs and – signs at the conclusion.

   1. My parent(s) or caregiver(s) attended college.

   2. I attended college.

   3. I have never skipped a meal because there was no food in the house.

   4. I am a white man.

   5. I have all of my cognitive and physical abilities.

   6. I have a college degree.

   7. I attended an elite university.

   8. I was born in the United States.

   9. English is my first language.

10. I never have felt passed over for a job based on your gender, ethnicity, age or sexual orientation.

11. I do not feel excluded from key social or networking opportunities because of your gender, ethnicity, age or sexual orientation.

12. I have not been asked to do menial office tasks that colleagues of another gender are not asked to do.

13. I can speak openly about my significant other.

14. I feel I can actively & effectively contribute to meetings you attend.

15. I have recently received feedback about a skill I need to grow my career.

16. I can talk about politically-oriented extra-curricular activities without fear of judgment from colleagues.

17. I have a partner who takes on a large share of household and family responsibilities.

18. I have never been called a "diversity hire."

19. I have never been mistaken as a member of the catering staff at an event.

20. I have never received an unwanted sexual advance at work.

21. I feel safe being my full self at work.

22. I am not concerned about losing my job because of my financial situation.

23. I haven't been able to join in out-of-office lunches or after-work social activities because of the cost.

24. I grew up with a computer in the home.

25. I read story books as a kid with characters who looked like me.

26. I grew up with mayors, politicians - a president - who looked like me.

27. I can walk past a construction site w/o being stared at + catcalled.

28. I was not embarrassed as child to have friends at my home.

29. I go to meetings where people look like me.

30. I have friends at work that look and think like me.

___ Total – signs   ___ Total + signs

2. When you finish, process these questions:

    a. What shifted for you?

    b. How are you seeing your life differently now?

    c. How can you start to use your privilege for positive change?

    d. What statements were surprising to see on this list as indicators of privilege?

Privilege Group / Class Activity

Objective: Group members will understand their privilege and begin to process how they can use it for good.

Materials:

— Kids' version of the Privilege Inventory
— Some kind of item the kids can have such as plastic coins, M&Ms, blocks, etc. You will want two different colors. About 20 of each color per child. (If this isn't feasible, google search for "Blank counting boxes" or "Blank number chart" and you can have kids use two different colors of writing utensils and color in the boxes as you say the statements.)

Directions:

1. Once you have completed the privilege exercise activity on your own, lead your group through this version. You will probably want to do this together so everyone understands each statement.

2. Say: "The purpose of this activity is for you to get a better understanding of your sources of privilege. Privilege is like an advantage you have. It's usually something you didn't earn– you have it just because of where you were born, how you grew up, what you look like, and other things you didn't control. Privilege is not a bad thing; it is a chance to be an ally for someone different than you. I am going to read each statement and if it is true for you, you will put a _____ colored item on your desk. If it isn't true for you, you will put a _____ colored item on your desk. At the end, we will look at how many of each color we have."

   a. Alternatively, if you aren't using manipulatives, you can say, "I am going to read each statement and if it is true for you, you will color the box _____. If it is not true for you, you will color the box _____. In the end, we will have 23 boxes colored on our sheet."
   b. As you read each statement, you'll want to remind them of what the colors stand for.

3. Read and discuss each statement with your class.

4. Have the kids count their coins on their desk or count the number of each color they have colored in their boxes.

5. Discuss these questions:
    a. What was surprising to you?
    b. Was there anything on the list that you thought everyone else experienced too? Something you thought was "normal" for all kids.
    c. How does this make you live or think differently now?

1. My parent(s) or caregiver(s) attended college.
2. I have never skipped a meal because there was no food in the house.
3. I am a white male.
4. I have all of my cognitive and physical abilities.
5. I am in school with majority of students and teachers who look like me.
6. I am able to attend any school Ii want.
7. My parents talk about me going to college one day.
8. I was born in the United States.
9. English is my first language.
10. I never have felt passed over for a sport or activity based on my gender, ethnicity, age or sexual orientation.
11. I do not feel excluded from friendships or social events because of my gender, ethnicity, age or sexual orientation.
12. I can speak openly about my parents/family.
13. I feel I can actively speak up in class.
14. I feel safe being my full self at school.
15. I am not concerned about my parents because of their financial situation.
16. I haven't had to say "no" to a social situation because my parents couldn't pay for it.
17. I have a computer in the home.
18. I read story books with characters who look like me.
19. I watch movies and television shows with lead characters who look like me.
20. I see mayors, politicians - a president - who looks like me.
21. I am not embarrassed to have friends at my home.
22. I go to activities and sports where people look like me.
23. I have friends at school that look and talk like me.

Privilege Group / Class Activity

Objective: Group members will identify and discuss situations involving racism.

Materials:

— A computer, phone or smart TV with access to Youtube
— Barbie Racism Video (To find this video, search on YouTube for 'barbie racism video')

Directions:

1. Watch the Barbie Racism video together as a group.

2. Discuss the following questions together:

    a. What situations were unfair? Why?

    b. How would you respond to a friend if they shared things like that?

    c. What could you do to prevent or stop things like that happening to people in your life?

Privilege Group / Class Activity

Objective: Kids will understand the gender pay gap and discuss solutions.

Materials:

— Some materials to build (blocks, legos, cups, etc.)
— Some materials to count (coins, blocks, markers, etc.)
— Some materials to sort (markers, crayons, colored manipulatives, toys, etc.)
— Some kind of reward (a type of candy, fake money, etc.)

Directions:

1. Choose 3 boys and 3 girls. Before you begin, know that you will be rewarding the boys more for the work they do in this activity because you will be discussing and helping the kids understand the gender pay gap.

2. Assign a boy and a girl to build something. Say: "Your job is to build whatever you want to build. You each have the exact same tools to use. You can start whenever you're ready. You'll each earn a reward for your work."

3. Assign a boy and a girl to count the counting materials you gave. Say: "Your job is to count these materials I have given you. When you've counted them, write how many there are on a piece of paper and don't show it to the other person. You'll each earn a reward for your work."

4. Assign a boy and a girl to sort the items you have chosen. Say: "These items need to be sorted. You can decide how you sort them, but they all need to be sorted. You will each receive a reward for your work when you finish."

5. Allow each group to finish before you give your rewards. Give the boys an obviously (but not too much) bigger reward. Allow the boys and girls to react.

6. Bring the group together for a discussion:

    a. What did you notice?

    b. Why do you think the boys got a better reward?

    c. Were the boys' and girls' jobs the same?

    d. Did you know that all over the world, women get paid less than men for doing the exact same job?

    e. What do you think about that?

    f. What would you do to fix this?

    g. If you let the kids keep their reward, make sure to give the girls the same amount as the boys in the end.

CHAPTER TEN – INSPIRATION

Inspiration Adult / Instructor Activity

Ally Vision Journal

1. Find a way to keep a journal and a way to process regularly with someone you trust in your life. Reflect on these questions as you consider your DEI journey:

   a. What is going well in your journey?

   b. How are you becoming a better ally for others?

   c. How are you diversifying your network?

   d. How are you having more candid conversations about DEI?

   e. What differences have you noticed with people in your life around DEI?

Inspiration Group / Class Activity

Objective: Group members will continue the conversation of diversity, equity, inclusion and allyship throughout their lives so that it begins to become normal and consistent.

Materials:

— The following list of questions printed off and saved

Directions:

1. Use the following list of questions and conversation starters to keep the conversation about DEI and allyship consistent in your group. Everytime your group gathers, ask a question or two at the beginning or end of the meeting. Or, you can tweak the questions a bit and use them to discuss a book you read, a video you watch together, or an exercise you do together as a group.

    a. Were you an ally to someone today? Tell me about it.

    b. Did you see someone getting bullied and treated badly today? Tell me about it.

    c. Who did you play with today? What did you do together?

    d. Is there anyone new you want to invite over to our house?

    e. What do you wish people understood about you? What do you want me to know about you?

    f. Was there a time you felt like you couldn't be yourself? Or was there a time you felt like you needed to change part of yourself? Tell me about it.

    g. Pick someone who you want to make their day. Let's talk about how we can do that!

EXTRA ACTIVITIES

Group / Class Activity

What I Wish My Teacher/Leader/Parent Knew

Objective: Teach children vulnerability by sharing vulnerable information about yourself and inviting them to do the same.

Materials:

- Pieces of paper
- Writing utensils
- "What I wish my students/kids knew" letter that you wrote to them, sharing what you would like to share.
    - Feel free to add any details you want to add. They can be funny, shocking, vulnerable, mundane, etc. I recommend including a variety of thoughts to give kids the confidence to do the same.

Directions:

1. Say: "Have you ever thought something about another person, and then realized you were totally wrong? Maybe you thought another kid didn't like you, but really she was just shy and didn't know how to talk to you. Maybe you thought your mom was mad at you, but really she just had a bad day and it had nothing to do with you. Maybe you noticed your friend is sad about losing a game at recess, but really his parents were going through a divorce and he was carrying that sadness with him. It's helpful in our relationships with one another, if we are able to be open and honest. We can seek to understand each other so that we know how to be kind to one another. The better we know someone, the less we are inclined to hate or be hurtful towards others."

2. Say: "Have you ever noticed that sometimes teachers and students or adults and kids can sometimes misunderstand each other? Maybe you get in trouble for something and you feel like the adult didn't understand the real situation. Today, we are going to do an activity that helps us share what's really on our minds and hearts so that we can better understand

each other. First, I am going to share a letter I wrote to you so you can see what we are doing."

3. Read the letter you wrote. Once you're finished, you may want to explain why you decided to share some of what you shared (if it wasn't obvious in the letter).

4. Say: "Now it's your turn. You will write a letter to me finishing this thought: 'What I wish you really knew about me.' And you can be free to share with me whatever you would like to share. I will be the only one reading this letter, so you don't have to worry about what you share being shared with anyone else."

5. Give kids time to write their letters. I recommend allowing them to spread out across the room if you can so that they have their own space to write.

6. Once kids turn in the letters, use them to help you care for each child individually as long as you have them. Follow up as you see necessary.

Group / Class Activity

Positive Self-Talk

Objective: Teach children how to speak positive affirmations over themselves and practice doing it.

Materials:

- Blank 9 piece puzzle (do a Google search for "Printable 9 piece puzzle template")
- Coloring utensils
- Writing utensil that is thin – pen or thin marker
- Whiteboard or some kind of big piece of paper that the whole class can see
- Scissors
- Sandwich bags

Directions:

1. Say: "Have you ever felt sad or frustrated because you felt like you couldn't accomplish something, you lost in a game, you didn't do the best you could, or anything like that? Tell me about that time in your life."

2. Say: "In those times, and a lot of times, it's easy for us to listen to the negative thoughts that pop into our heads. Everyone struggles with this. Even adults. We listen to negative thoughts like: 'I'm not good enough,' 'I'll never win,' 'I can't do it,' 'No one likes me.' But we can overcome those negative thoughts by learning how to talk to ourselves positively instead of listen to those negative thoughts. It can sound like this: 'I can do this,' 'I'm a leader,' 'I am capable,' 'I can do this with the help of others,' 'I am enough.' Let's make a list together of all of the positive things we can start saying to each other."

3. Make a list of positive self-talk/affirmations together.

4. Say: "We're going to do a craft together that will help us remember these positive things to say to ourselves. And we can pull it out any time we need to remember these things."

5. Pass out the puzzles (don't cut yet.)

6. Pass out the thin writing utensils.

7. Say: "On each puzzle piece, you'll write a positive affirmation. Pick from the list we created together. Pick ones that you really want to believe and say over yourself. Once you've written the positive self-talk, color the pieces however you would like."

8. Pass out the coloring utensils when kids have written the positive affirmations.

9. Allow time to write affirmations and color. Walk around the room and talk about what they've written and why.

10. Pass out scissors and allow them to cut out their puzzle pieces.

11. Say: "Now, try to put your puzzle back together. As you do, say those affirmations out loud to yourself."

12. Pass out baggies for kids to put their pieces inside. You can choose to keep the puzzles in your group space and pull them out whenever kids need some positive self-talk, or you can have them take them home.

Adult / Instructor Activity

Helping Children & Teens Manage Stress

1. Read <u>this article</u> (Google search: "How to Help Children and Teens Manage Stress, NEA.org.)

2. Talk about the following questions with another adult who often works with the same kids you do, or talk to your spouse as this applies to your own children.

    a. Read the signs of stress from the beginning of the article. What signs have you/are you seeing in your children/class? When do you see these signs of stress or what situation(s) have they come about?

    b. Read the list of stress management solutions. What seems to be lacking for your children/class? What seems to be going well?

    c. Pick something from the list that you'd like to start implementing in your child's/class's routine. Talk about how you can start to implement it together.

    d. Read the three ways caregivers can help.

        i. In what ways have you allowed your kids/class to be problem-solvers? In what ways have you solved the problem yourself?

        ii. In what ways have you promoted media literacy? In what ways can you better promote media literacy?

        iii. In what ways are you hearing negative thinking from your child/class? In what ways have you perpetuated it by speaking negatively about yourself and others? In what ways can you be better about promoting positive thinking? What can you start to implement that helps your children/class practice positive thinking so that it becomes a habit?

Adult / Instructor Activity

The Real Rosa Parks

1. Listen to this podcast: <u>The Real Rosa Parks and the Montgomery Bus Boycott</u>. (Do a Google search for the title. It is on Learningforjustice.org). This podcast teaches more in-depth about Rosa Parks and what truly took place on December 1, 1955. Answer the following questions on your own or talk about them with a friend as you listen together.

2. Before listening: How do you picture Rosa Parks when you think about her? What kind of person is she? What is her temperament/demeanor? What do you know about Rosa Parks and the Montgomery Bus Boycott? In what settings did you learn about her?

3. After listening: How are you seeing Rosa Parks differently? What new things did you learn? Why do you think you haven't learned these things about her until today? How is history told differently depending on who is teaching it?

4. Use what you have learned to teach your group/family/class so that they can then share with others as well.

    a. Here are some books that you can use to help teach about Rosa Parks for children:
        i. So Other People Would Be Also Free: The Real Story of Rosa Parks for Kids by Tonya Leslie, PH.D (ages 8-12)
        ii. A Picture Book of Rosa Parks by David A. Adler (ages 6+)
        iii. If a Bus Could Talk: The Story of Rosa Parks by Faith Ringgold (ages 6+)
        iv. When Rosa Parks Went Fishing by Rachel Ruiz (ages 6+)

Group / Class Activity

Personal Development Activity

Objective: Children will practice skills used for personal growth and development through goal-setting.

Materials:

- Pieces of paper
- Writing utensils/coloring utensils
- Foldable booklets (do a Google search for "foldable booklet template" and choose one that works for your group. You'll want about 4 pages.)

Directions:

1. Discuss: "What is something you are good at? How did you get good at that? What is something you want to be better at? When we want to learn to be better at something, what are some things we can do to get better or grow?"

2. Say: "When we want to get better at something we never magically get better. You can't just say, 'I want to be a better soccer player' and do nothing to try to get better. You wouldn't wake up one day a better soccer player. It's the same way with learning to be a better ally for others. We can't just say we want to be better ally and hope we will wake up better. It's important to set goals and take action to reach those goals."

3. Discuss: "What is something you're good at when it comes to being an ally for others?" (you may need to help them come up with different parts of their personalities or skill sets that make them good allies. For example, they're empathetic, inclusive, observant, they're good at asking questions, they're good at inviting, etc.)

4. Discuss: "What is something you want to be better at when it comes to being an ally? Think about your long-term goal. Thinking about the future, what do you want to do for others as an ally?"

5. Pass out pieces of paper and have the kids write down their goal. They could draw it, write it, etc.

6. Discuss: "In what ways can you take action to reach that goal?"

7. Pass out the booklets (or templates and work together to put together the booklets)

    a. On the front have them create a title page that says something like "Personal Ally Growth."

    b. The first page is their long-term goal. Have them write/draw their long-term goal of what it would look like for them to grow in being an ally.

8. Discuss: "What are little bits of action you can take to reach that goal?" (You may need to help them come up with little steps of action that they can take each day/week to reach that goal. This could be anything like reaching out to a specific friend each day, asking their friends a specific question or reading a new book/watching a show that teaches them about others.)

    a. Help each child come up with about 3 action steps. Have them dedicate one page per action step.

    b. This is a good time for kids to talk to each other as they create theirs so that they can share ideas and goals. This will help them learn how to talk about their own goals so that it becomes normal/habitual.

9. Frequently reference their goals throughout your time together. Try talking about them weekly first. Here are some questions to ask to get students thinking about their goals consistently:

    a. How are you doing with your goal?

    b. Tell me about the action steps you took this week to work toward your goal.

    c. Tell me about why you haven't taken action steps this week if you haven't.

    d. What has been getting in the way of taking action toward your goal?

    e. What has been helping you take action toward your goal?

Group / Class Activity
(To then be implemented in groups)

Windows and Mirrors

1. Read this article to learn about Mirrors, Windows and Sliding Glass Doors (do a Google search for "What are Windows, Mirrors, and Sliding Glass Doors? – WeAreTeachers.")

2. Then, watch this video to see some of those ideas in action (search on YouTube for "Windows and Mirrors: Learning about Difference - and belonging - through books.")

3. Take a look around your group space. Are there posters, pictures, phrases, etc. that are mirrors and windows? How might you create more windows and mirrors with the physical space (if you are able)?

4. Look through the books and learning materials available to your kids in your space. Are there many different windows and mirrors so that kids can see themselves, but also learn about others? How might you add more books and learning materials to diversify your collection?

5. Browse through the lists of resources at the end of the article. If you are able, consider which books would be beneficial to include in your group's book collection.

6. Here is a list of different questions you can ask as you read books that are windows/mirrors. It is good to stop a few times throughout the book and ask questions. Point to characters and ask kids to engage in the illustrations. Get students discussing and connecting to the characters and story as a whole.

   a. Put your finger on your nose if you have ever felt like this character.
   b. Put your finger on your nose up if you've experienced something similar.
   c. Thumbs up every time you see a character that looks like you.
   d. What do you think this character is feeling?
   e. What do you think this character might be thinking?
   f. What do you think the other characters think of this character?

g. What would you do if you were in their situation?

h. What is something new you learned from this book?

i. Were any of the characters like you in any way?

j. How were the characters different from you?

k. What is a new way you are thinking/a new idea you have because of this book?

l. How did this book help you with your own life/situation?

ADDITIONAL RESOURCES

Organizations & Activities

Learning for Justice (https://www.learningforjustice.org/), a project of the Southern Poverty Law Center, provides classroom resources to help bring relevance, rigor and social emotional learning into classrooms. Also check out their professional development resources and magazine.

Moms Against Racism (https://www.momsagainstracism.org/) is a member based non-profit organization that is operated throughout the USA. Their mission is to unify parenting skills while teaching anti-racism by doing the work, starting at home. They are a pillar within their respective communities and serve education systems, workplaces and youth by advocating for anti-racist practices emphasizing diversity & inclusion. Get involved and check out virtual classes and engagement opportunities!

Doing Good Together's (https://www.doinggoodtogether.org/dgts-antiracist-resource-collection) mission is unique and deeply layered. They provide tools to both families and organizations to help them raise compassionate, engaged children. Their innovative activities, resources, and support help make empathy and "giving back" a natural part of life's early lessons. Check out their robust resource list of Tools to Raise an Anti-Racist Generation!

BrainPOP (https://blog.brainpop.com/antiracist-education-free-resources-kids/) is committed to combating racism by creating content that examines the long and painful history of race in America. Check out this list of topics, recommended by grade level, to help engage in these difficult but essential conversations.

Kids That Do Good (https://kidsthatdogood.com/about/) was created by Jake and Max, twin brothers from New Jersey who were frustrated that they could not volunteer in certain areas due to their young age. Kids That Do Good is an online resource for kids, and their families, to get involved with existing charities as well as create their own ways to give back.

TeenVogue's (https://www.teenvogue.com/tag/diversity) archive of articles focused on Diversity - offering excellent, timely resources for your teens.

The Fairplay book and **Cards by Eve Rodsky** (https://www.fairplaylife.com/the-cards-1) are a couple's conversation guide that will help adults rebalance to-do lists, reclaim time, and rediscover and nurture the skills and interests that make you uniquely you. Ultimately these guides set couples up for success in their relationship and parenting and create equality in a relationship, a great activity to model for your children.

University of Michigan Inclusive Teaching is an excellent resource for group and classroom activities providing innovative teaching methods and tools that foster success for students through inclusive teaching practices. The following are excellent activities:

- Personal Identity Wheel
- Social Identity Wheel
- The Spectrum Activity, Questions of Identity
- Mapping Social Identity Timeline Activity
- Invisible Knapsacks - To help students understand the concept of white privilege
- Racial Bias Test
- Examining Privilege and Oppression

Local Organizations to Engage Within Specific Geographies:

Seeds of Caring (https://www.seedsofcaring.org/about) believes in the power of kindness and the capacity for kids to change the world. They engage children ages 2-12—our future leaders—through a variety of service, social action, and community-building experiences. From racism to homelessness, they don't shy away from the tough stuff. Instilling kindness and empathy from the earliest age, Seeds of Caring helps kids see and understand the needs in their community, then develop the social-emotional skills and confidence to make a difference. Partnering with over 40 non-profit organizations in the **Central Ohio** area, they connect caring children and families with service and community-building opportunities focused on: Homelessness & Hunger, Systemic Racism, Stigmas Surrounding Developmental Disabilities and LGBTQ+, Senior Isolation & Loneliness, and Environmental Care.

The Honeycomb Project (https://www.thehoney combproject.org/justice-curriculum) puts kids at the forefront of social change. The Honeycomb Project engages, mobilizes, and inspires whole families to build strong and connected communities through service. Live programs take place in **Chicago**, but the Honeycomb project also has a virtual volunteer program designed to uplift and mobilize kids during these uncertain times. Honeycomb is offering free online lessons featuring inspiring videos, dinner discussion topics, enriching volunteer activities, and more. Check out their Civic Engagement & Social Justice at-home projects!

Pint Size Protesters (https://pintsizeprotesters.org/), Located in **Central Ohio**, is committed to raising anti-racist children and educating the next generation of social justice warriors. They believe that Black Lives Matter and their mission is to give kids and families a safe space in the movement by organizing, educating, and demonstrating.

Pebble Tossers (https://www.pebbletossers.org/), located in **Atlanta, Georgia** is a youth development nonprofit with a mission to empower and equip youth to lead through service.

Generation Serve (https://www.generationserve.org/), located in **Austin and Houston, Texas,** has a mission to engage children in volunteerism and empower them to make a difference in their communities. Check out their in person and virtual family volunteer activities.

Know of other excellent local organizations to include for kids volunteerism opportunities? Let us know at nextpivotpoint.com/contact

Books

- *The Cycle of a Dream: A Kid's Introduction to Structural Racism in America* by Kimberly Narain – "Each page walks you through the history of social injustice, inequalities and racism in America. However, this book also shares a very positive message that can become a conversation piece with family, friends or in the classroom."

- *I Promise* by LeBron James - NBA champion and superstar LeBron James pens a slam-dunk picture book inspired by his foundation's I PROMISE program that motivates children everywhere to always #StriveForGreatness. Just a kid from Akron, Ohio, who is dedicated to uplifting youth everywhere, LeBron James knows the key to a better future is to excel in school, do your best, and keep your family close. *I Promise* is a lively and inspiring picture book that reminds us that tomorrow's success starts with the promises we make to ourselves and our community today.

- *Julián Is a Mermaid* by Jessica Love – A glimpse of costumed mermaids leaves one boy floored with wonder and ready to dazzle the world. Julián is a Mermaid is a story about a boy and his Abuela. It is a story about being seen for who we are by someone who loves us.

- *My Mom Has Two Jobs* by Michelle Travis – Finally, a children's picture book that pays homage to working moms everywhere! My Mom Has Two Jobs celebrates the work that women do both inside and outside of the home.

- *My Heart Fills With Happiness by Monique Gray Smith* – A book to support the wellness of Indegenous children and families and to encourage young children to reflect on what makes them happy.

- *Change Sings: A Children's Anthem by Amanda Gorman* – In this stirring, much-anticipated picture book by presidential inaugural poet and activist Amanda Gorman, anything is possible when our voices join together. As a young girl leads a cast of characters on a musical journey, they learn that they have the power to make changes—big or small—in the world, in their communities, and most importantly, in themselves.

- *Guji-Guji by Chih-Yuan Chen* – Guji Guji is just your ordinary, everyday, run-of-the-mill duck…um, crocodile…um, duck… In this engaging story about identity, loyalty and what it really means to be a family, Guji, Guji makes some pretty big decisions about who he is, what he is, and what it all means, anyway.

- *The Adventures of Bug and Boo-Under the Sea by Denay Hooks* – Bug has a rare disease and uses a wheelchair, but when she and her brother are on these adventures, she is able to do things her body doesn't typically allow. They swim with colorful fish, find an old pirate ship, and still manage to make it home by dinner.

- *A Zebra Named Zion by Ben Smith* – A simple story designed to provoke discussion about mental health in primary school aged children.

- *Just Ask!: Be Different, Be Brave, Be You by Sonia Sotomayor* – US Supreme Court Justice Sonia Sotomayor celebrates the different abilities kids (and people of all ages) have.

- *When Charley Met Emma by Amy Webb* – This book will help kids think about disability, kindness and how to behave when they meet someone who is different from them.

- *Journey To Appleville by Veronica Appleton* – What can six kids from a local neighborhood do when they have a goal in mind? Embark on a quest to Appleville, of course! Join Kenan, Tu-Tu, Pedro, Liu-Liu, Lizzy, and Cassie as they overcome their fears with the help of the Appleville Fairy.

- *Hear My Voice/Escucha mi voz by Warren Binford* – The Testimonies of Children Detained at the Southern Border of the United States.

- *Born Ready – THE TRUE STORY OF A BOY NAMED PENELOPE by JODIE PATTERSON* – Jodie Patterson, activist and Chair of the Human Rights Campaign Foundation Board, shares her transgender son's experience in this important picture book about identity and acceptance.

- *Milo Imagines the World by MATT DE LA PEÑA* – Milo and his teen sister, who are both Black, take a long subway ride together. Big sister is glued to her cell phone and bespectacled Milo draws the lives he imagines for other passengers on the train.

- *Call and Response: The Story of Black Lives Matter* by Veronica Chambers – a broad and powerful exploration of the history of Black Lives Matter told through photographs, quotes, and informative text.

- *We Are Still Here! Native American Truths Everyone Should Know* by Traci Sorell – Twelve Native American kids present historical and contemporary laws, policies, struggles, and victories in Native life, each with a powerful refrain: We are still here!

- *Eyes that Kiss in the Corners* by Joanna Ho – A young Taiwanese girl notices that her eyes look different from her friends'. This book is a dazzling, lyrical ode to loving oneself.

- *Rescue & Jessica* by Jessica Kensky – A young woman who has lost her leg finds a helpful companion in Rescue, her new service dog, in this story based on the author's experience after losing both legs due to injuries received in the 2013 Boston Marathon bombing.

- *Henry the Boy* by Molly Felder – No matter how different we feel, we are all more similar than we at first appear. This is not a story about a heron or a robot or a chicken but an ordinary boy with daily struggles, triumphs, and an extraordinary imagination.

- *When Stars Are Scattered* by Victoria Jamieson, Omar Mohamed – A graphic novel about growing up in a refugee camp, as told by a former Somali refugee.

- *All the Way to the Top: How One Girl's Fight for Americans with Disabilities Changed Everything* by Annette Bay Pimentel – Experience the true story of lifelong activist Jennifer Keelan-Chaffins and her participation in the Capitol Crawl in this inspiring autobiographical picture book.

- *Not My Idea: A Book about Whiteness* by Anastasia Higginbotham – a picture book about racism and racial justice, inviting white children and parents to become curious about racism, accept that it's real, and cultivate justice.

- *Chocolate Me!* by Taye Diggs – A timely book about how it feels to be teased and taunted, and how each of us is sweet and lovely and delicious on the inside, no matter how we look.

- *My Hair Is a Garden* by Cozbi A. Cabrera – After a day of being taunted by classmates about her unruly hair, Mackenzie can't take any more and she seeks guidance from her wise and comforting neighbor, Miss Tillie. Using the beautiful garden in the backyard as a metaphor, Miss Tillie shows Mackenzie that maintaining healthy hair is not a chore nor is it something to fear. Most importantly, Mackenzie learns that natural black hair is beautiful.

- *The Day You Begin* by Jacqueline Woodson – a poignant, yet heartening book about finding courage to connect, even when you feel scared and alone. There will be times when you walk into a room and no one there is quite like you…

- *Separate Is Never Equal: Sylvia Mendez and Her Family's Fight for Desegregation* by Duncan Tonatiuh – Seven years before Brown v. Board of Education, the Mendez family fought to end segregation in California schools. Discover their incredible story in this picture book from award-winning creator Duncan Tonatiuh.

- *Skin Again* by Bell Hooks – a new way to talk about race and identity that will appeal to parents of the youngest readers. The skin I'm in is just a covering. It cannot tell my story. If you want to know who I am, you have got to come inside and open your heart way wide.

- *As Brave as You* by Jason Reynolds – a book that explores multigenerational ideas about family love and bravery in the story of two brothers, their blind grandfather, and a dangerous rite of passage.

You can find additional resources at inclusionschool.com/resources

JULIE KRATZ: SPEAKER / TRAINER / AUTHOR

Julie Kratz is a highly acclaimed TEDx speaker and inclusive leadership trainer who led teams and produced results in corporate America. After experiencing many career "pivot points" of her own, she started her own speaking business with the goal of helping leaders be more inclusive. Promoting diversity, inclusion, and allyship in the workplace, Julie helps organizations foster more inclusive environments. She is a frequent keynote speaker, podcast host, and executive coach. She holds an MBA from the Kelley School of Business at Indiana University, is a Certified Master Coach, and is a Certified Unconscious Bias Trainer, and Certified in Social Emotional Learning (SEL).

Her books include *Pivot Point: How to Build a Winning Career Game Plan, ONE: How Male Allies Support Women for Gender Equality,* and *Lead Like an Ally: A Journey Through Corporate America with Strategies to Facilitate Inclusion,* and her new children's book and coloring book, "Little Allies."

Find Julie at NextPivotPoint.com, @NextPivotPoint, or on LinkedIn.

Made in the USA
Coppell, TX
29 June 2022

79356230R10040